The RIVER GROWS

Written by Gale Clifford
Photographed by Paul M. Dyer

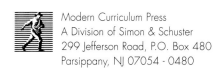

Modern Curriculum Press
A Division of Simon & Schuster
299 Jefferson Road, P.O. Box 480
Parsippany, NJ 07054 - 0480

Design and production by BIG BLUE DOT

ISBN: 0-8136-0815-5 Modern Curriculum Press

2 3 4 5 6 7 8 9 10 SP 01 00 99 98 97 96 95

The snow melts.

The river begins to grow.

The water drips down.

It slips down.

It spills over rocks.

The river grows.

The river flows.

Here the river is slow.

But here the river is fast.

It flows past tall trees.

It flows past green grass.

It doesn't stop.

It crashes down.

The river grows.

The river flows.

It flows into a bigger river.

Then the river meets the sea.